MIRACLES OF MEDICINE

GENE THERAPY

BY VIC KOVACS

Gareth Stevens
PUBLISHING

Please visit our website, www.garethstevens.com.
For a free color catalog of all our high-quality books, call toll free 1-800-542-2595 or fax 1-877-542-2596.

Cataloging-in-Publication Data

Names: Kovacs, Vic.
Title: Gene therapy / Vic Kovacs.
Description: New York : Gareth Stevens Publishing, 2017. | Series: Miracles of medicine | Includes index.
Identifiers: ISBN 9781482460995 (pbk.) | ISBN 9781482461688 (library bound) | ISBN 9781482460988 (6 pack)
Subjects: LCSH: Gene therapy--Juvenile literature.
Classification: LCC RB155.8 K68 2017 | DDC 615.8'95--dc23

Published in 2017 by
Gareth Stevens Publishing
111 East 14th Street, Suite 349
New York, NY 10003

Developed and produced for Rosen by BlueApple*Works* Inc.

Managing Editor for BlueAppleWorks: Melissa McClellan
Designer: Joshua Avramson
Photo Research: Jane Reid
Editor: Marcia Abramson

Photo Credits: Cover Andrew Brookes/Getty Images; Title page Monika Wisniewska/Shutterstock; p. 5 Linda Bucklin/
Shutterstock; p. 6 /Public Domain; p. 7 Marjorie McCarty/Creative Commons; p. 8 Wellcome Images/Creative Commons;
p. 9 Fnorman-london/Creative Commons; p. 11 vitstudio/Shutterstock; p. 12 Sashkin/Shutterstock; p. 13 background
everything possible/Shutterstock; p. 13 NoPainNoGain /Shutterstock; p. 15, 28 Tyler Olson /Shutterstock; p. 16 Dietmar
Temps/Shutterstock.com; p. 17, 31 Alexander Raths /Shutterstock; p. 19 Matej Kastelic/Shutterstock; p. 22 Mopic/
Shutterstock; p. 23 PHB.cz (Richard Semik) /Shutterstock; p. 25 Russ London at English Wikipedia/Creative Commons;
p. 27 Romanova Natali; p. 33 Monkey Business Images/Shutterstock; p. 34 Sebastian Kaulitzki /Shutterstock; p. 35
nobeastsofierce/Shutterstock; p. 37 Photographee.eu /Shutterstock; p. 38 Diego Cervo /Shutterstock; p. 39 frantab/
Shutterstock; p. 42 National Institutes of Health/Creative Commons

Printed in the United States of America

CPSIA compliance information: Batch CW17GS: For further information contact Gareth Stevens, New York, New York at 1-800-542-2595.

CONTENTS

CHAPTER 1

THE HISTORY OF GENE THERAPY

There are many different kinds of **diseases** that affect human beings. Many are caused by infections, when the body is invaded by foreign **organisms** such as **bacteria** or **viruses**. These can often be treated or prevented. Antibiotics have proven effective against bacteria, and vaccines are useful in stopping infection from many viruses and bacteria from occurring in the first place. Some diseases aren't caused by outside factors, though. Some diseases are caused by faulty genes that already exist in a person's body.

Genes are specific strands of DNA that act as instructions for your body. The whole DNA **molecule** is called a chromosome, and humans have 23 pairs of these chromosomes. Taken together, these chromosomes are what make you the unique person you are.

DNA PACKAGE

IN ORDER TO FIT INSIDE A CELL, DNA WINDS TIGHTLY INTO STRUCTURES CALLED CHROMOSOMES. IF DNA FROM A SINGLE HUMAN CELL WAS UNRAVELED, IT WOULD BE SIX FEET LONG!

Human evolution likely began in Africa about six million years ago. Through a long series of advantageous DNA changes, humans became differentiated from our ancestors in the ape family.

DNA AND EVOLUTION

Understanding DNA has helped scientists decipher evolution. In recent years, the genomes of almost all species have been mapped and digitized. By comparing these genomes, scientists can tell how species overlap genetically and where and when they differentiated. Certain proteins are needed by all living species, so there is a great deal of overlap, but species that are closely related show the most similarities. The DNA difference between human beings and our closest simian relatives, the chimps and bonobos, is about 1.2 percent. Gorillas are more distant cousins at a 1.6 percent difference. The difference between individual humans, meanwhile, is only about 0.1 percent. It's even possible now to track the history of those differences by DNA analysis, which can pinpoint an individual's ancestral roots.

Genes are made up of specific sequences of DNA that tell your body how to make a specific **protein**. Each protein determines a different aspect of your body. For example, one gene might be responsible for making the protein that makes your eyes blue. Another might be responsible for how tall you grow. Chromosomes, and the genes and DNA they're made up of, are hereditary. That means they're passed down from parents to their children. Every single cell in your body has two sets of 23 chromosomes, one from each parent.

Some people have genes that don't work the way they're supposed to. Most people have genes that tell their blood how to clot and close a wound when they're cut. However, some people's genes don't carry the correct instructions, so when they're cut, they just keep bleeding. This is called hemophilia, and it's an example of what's called a genetic disorder, or genetic disease.

DNA was first discovered by a Swiss scientist named Frederich Miescher in 1869. While trying to identify the proteins that made up white blood cells, he came across a previously unknown substance.

Frederich Miescher (1844–1895), who discovered DNA, came from a family of doctors and scientists.

Many scientists were trying, but James Watson (left) and Francis Crick (1916–2004) were the first to decipher the double helix of DNA.

Miescher called this substance "nuclein," which would later be changed to "nucleic acid," and then to "deoxyribonucleic acid," which was shortened to DNA.

Researchers continued to investigate DNA throughout the first half of the 20th century. By the 1950s, it had been suggested that DNA was responsible for heredity, which is the passage of traits from parents to children. Scientists were hard at work to discover the exact structure of DNA so they could better understand how it worked. The mystery was solved by two American scientists named Francis Crick and James Watson in 1953. They figured out that DNA was a double helix, a kind of spiral made up of two chains of DNA winding around each other. Their findings would not have been possible without research done by Rosalind Franklin. Franklin had managed to take an X-ray photograph of a crystalline form of DNA. The photograph, which showed DNA as an X, was passed on to Crick and Watson by Franklin's colleague Maurice Wilkins.

This photograph led directly to their double helix theory. In 1962, Crick and Watson received the Nobel Prize for their discovery, which they shared with Wilkins. Franklin, who died in 1958, was not eligible.

As scientists began to understand exactly what DNA was and what it did, they began to look for medical uses for this knowledge. The idea of gene therapy was first proposed in 1972. It was theorized that faulty genes could be repaired or replaced by injecting cells with normal DNA that functions the way it's supposed to. The first human trial took place in 1980. During a trial to treat the blood disorder thalassemia, researcher Martin Cline had permission to inject two separate genes into his patients. However, he linked the two genes with a plasmid, a kind of circular DNA molecule. This type of procedure, where two separate genes are brought together in a laboratory, creates something called recombinant DNA, or rDNA. Cline was not cleared to use rDNA in his trials, and was found to be in violation of federal regulations. He was eventually sanctioned by the US National Institutes of Health.

Gene therapy is still one of the newest branches of medicine. Today, it's a mostly experimental treatment, and is usually only available in select clinical trials. It's also heavily regulated by governments, due to how risky it can be. As a result of these risks, it's generally only used for diseases with no other known cure.

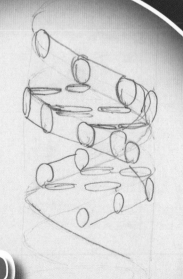

Francis Crick drew this pencil sketch in 1953 to illustrate the concept of the DNA double helix.

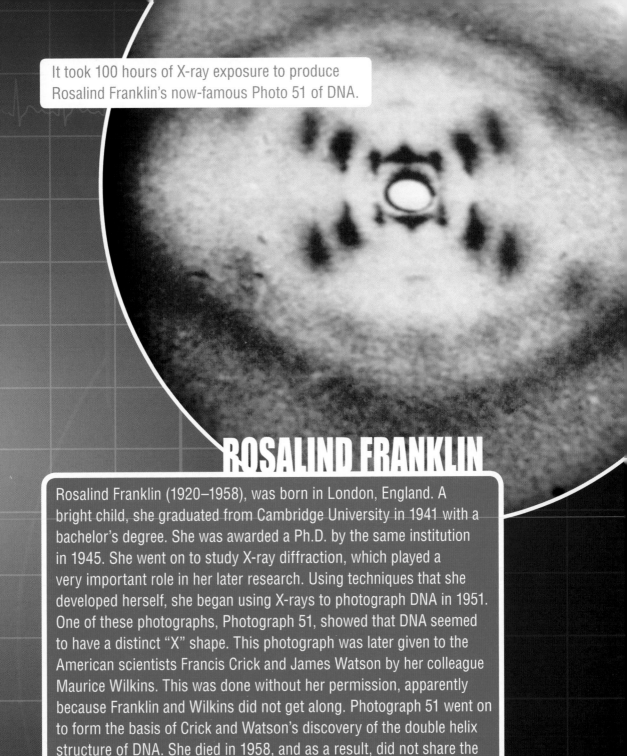

It took 100 hours of X-ray exposure to produce Rosalind Franklin's now-famous Photo 51 of DNA.

ROSALIND FRANKLIN

Rosalind Franklin (1920–1958), was born in London, England. A bright child, she graduated from Cambridge University in 1941 with a bachelor's degree. She was awarded a Ph.D. by the same institution in 1945. She went on to study X-ray diffraction, which played a very important role in her later research. Using techniques that she developed herself, she began using X-rays to photograph DNA in 1951. One of these photographs, Photograph 51, showed that DNA seemed to have a distinct "X" shape. This photograph was later given to the American scientists Francis Crick and James Watson by her colleague Maurice Wilkins. This was done without her permission, apparently because Franklin and Wilkins did not get along. Photograph 51 went on to form the basis of Crick and Watson's discovery of the double helix structure of DNA. She died in 1958, and as a result, did not share the Nobel Prize given to Crick, Watson, and Wilson for the discovery she was an integral part of in 1962.

THE MIGHTY DNA

Although scientists have known about DNA since 1869, it's only recently that we've begun to unlock its mysteries. Today, we know what DNA is and what it does, and we're also figuring out how to use that knowledge to help people!

DNA

DNA is a molecule that exists in every living thing on Earth. It carries the instructions for pretty much everything your body does. Some of these instructions are for cosmetic factors, such as the color of your hair, eyes, or skin.

DNA is composed of four different chemical bases. These are adenine (A), thymine (T), guanine (G), and cytosine (C). These bases are paired together to form pairs. A only pairs with T, and C only pairs with G.

INFORMATION IN A CELL

HUMAN BODIES HAVE 210 KINDS OF CELLS, EACH TYPE WITH A DIFFERENT TASK.
WITHIN THESE GROUPS, EACH INDIVIDUAL CELL FUNCTIONS LIKE A
MINI-COMPUTER USING DNA AS ITS SOFTWARE, OR INSTRUCTION CODE.

DNA can make exact copies of itself, which then pass on its traits to new cells. This process is called replication, and it happens before cells divide to make new ones. The strand of DNA must unwind, bit by bit, in order to serve as a pattern for the new strand, and then wind back up again.

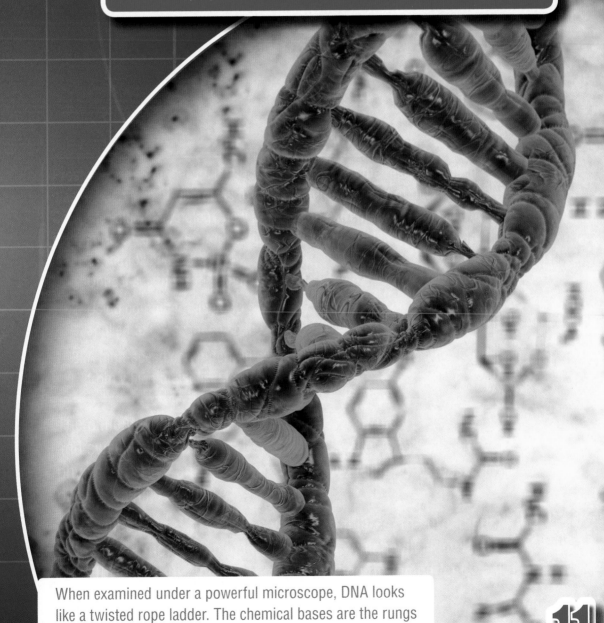

When examined under a powerful microscope, DNA looks like a twisted rope ladder. The chemical bases are the rungs while sugar and phosphorus molecules are the sides.

These base pairs are also attached to a sugar molecule and a phosphate molecule, which alternate. When linked together, these four ingredients are known as a nucleotide. The order of the four bases determines what exactly that sequence does. Each sequence responsible for a singe trait or purpose is called a gene. Genes are all part of a longer strand of DNA that makes up a double helix. These double helixes are able to split apart to reproduce, with each half strand becoming a new double helix. The whole double helix, made up of many different genes, is a chromosome.

If DNA is the instruction manual for everything our bodies do, how are those instructions read? First, **enzymes** decipher the information in a DNA molecule. They then "write" it onto another molecule, called a messenger ribonucleic acid, or mRNA. This molecule, as its name would suggest, then delivers its information, which is then "read" by the ribosome, the part of a cell that makes proteins. This information tells the cell which amino acids to put into specific sequences to make particular proteins. Every protein is made up of a different sequence of amino acids.

Chromosomes exist in the center, or nucleus, of every cell but they can be seen only with a high-powered microscope. Up close, they look like short worms.

Human mitochondria have a complex structure. Inside layers of membrane are 37 genes that regulate mitrochondrial functions.

MITOCHONDRIA

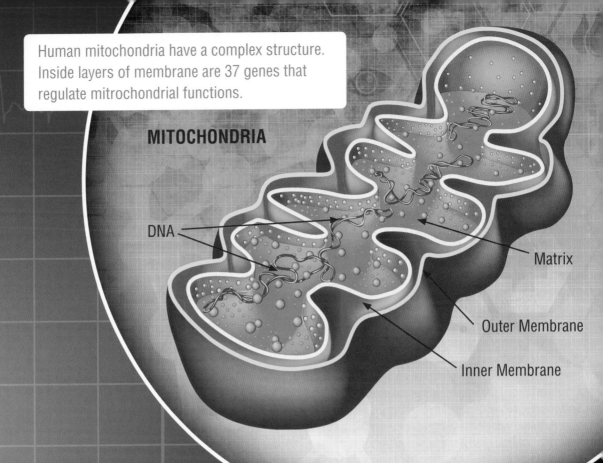

DNA

Matrix

Outer Membrane

Inner Membrane

MITOCHONDRIAL DNA

Like power plants, mitrochondria turn food into the energy that fuels cell function. They also play a role in cell signaling, growth, self-destruction, and production of some key substances such as iron in blood. Some simple cells have as few as two mitochondria while a complex cell with a demanding task, such as a muscle cell, has many more.

Mitochondria contain a small amount of their own DNA separate from the DNA packaged within the cell's chromosomes. This is called mtDNA (mitochondrial DNA). The mtDNA is passed on only from the mother in humans and almost all other species, so it can be used to trace a person's maternal heritage. It is also fairly easy to isolate and was the first major part of the human genome that researchers were able to sequence.

rDNA

Recombinant DNA, often shortened to rDNA, is made artificially, usually in a laboratory. It's made up of two or more gene sequences that are combined together. Often, the resulting rDNA strand does not exist in nature. Sometimes, it combines DNA strands from different species. For example, one rDNA strand might contain DNA from both a plant and a human.

Scientists create rDNA for a number of different purposes. One of the most important is research, where it's used to identify specific genes and their purposes. However, it's also hoped that specific rDNA strands can someday be constructed to be used in gene therapy, to help treat genetic disorders.

GENETIC DISORDERS

Genetic disorders or diseases are conditions that arise due to faulty genes in a genome. Many of these disorders begin at birth, but some only become noticeable with age. They're contracted in a few different ways. Some are hereditary, and others can occur due to a sudden **mutation** in a gene. These mutations themselves can then sometimes become hereditary. Some diseases, like cancer, might be hereditary in one person, and might be a spontaneous mutation in another.

Testing babies at birth helps families deal with some genetic disorders.

In some disorders, it's only necessary for one parent to have the **defective** gene to pass it on. For example, if one parent has the gene that causes Huntington's disease, but the other does not, there's a 50/50 chance their child will be born with the disease. Others require both parents to have a copy of the affected gene. In some of these cases, the gene might be recessive in both parents, meaning they won't show symptoms. In these cases, the parents are known as carriers.

DIAGNOSING A GENETIC DISORDER

There are many different kinds of genetic disorders, so diagnoses are widely varied. Because so many genetic diseases are hereditary, an extensive family history is one of the most useful diagnostic tools. If someone's ancestors have been known to suffer from a particular disorder, that helps to eliminate other, less likely possibilities.

People with albinism have pale, sensitive skin, so they must stay out of the sun. This genetic condition can affect people of every race and many animals, including penguins!

However, if the disease is caused by a new mutation, family history will not be of much help. Physical examinations also play an important role, as many disorders have fairly obvious physical symptoms. One example would be albinism, a disorder in which pigment is absent from the skin, hair, and eyes. As a result, an albino person has very pale skin and hair, and very light blue eyes.

Genetic tests can also reveal the presence of a genetic disorder. Today, most newborns in the United States are immediately screened for several different diseases. This is done early so that treatment can begin as soon as possible if a disorder is found. People trying to have children are also often screened to determine if one or both are carriers. If they are, they can then choose alternate methods of having a baby, such as in vitro fertilization, or adoption. Testing is also available for **fetuses**, to determine if they are developing normally, or for people of any age who might be predisposed to developing a disorder. One example would be for someone whose parent developed Huntington's disease after they were born.

A simple blood test tells people whether they are carriers of the defective gene that causes Tay-Sachs disease.

TAY-SACHS DISEASE

Tay-Sachs, a rare disorder, may disappear someday because of increased understanding of genetics and gene therapy.

Babies with classic Tay-Sachs disease lose their ability to hear, see, and move before dying at an early age. Tay-Sachs also has a slower juvenile form and a milder adult-onset form.

A defective gene causes Tay-Sachs, which is named for two doctors who first described it. People who have one copy of the gene do not get sick, but if both parents are carriers, their child may receive two copies of the gene and develop Tay-Sachs.

Tay-Sachs usually occurs in people with Jewish, French-Canadian, Louisiana Cajun, or Pennsylvania Dutch ancestry. Since the late 1960s, genetic testing has been available to identify carriers, who can then avoid passing on the gene, and the number of cases has declined. Scientists also are making progress in developing genetics-based therapies to slow down or someday even cure Tay-Sachs when it does occur.

CHAPTER 3
GENE THERAPY

Gene therapy holds the promise of a new kind of medicine, but it has a long way to go. Many scientists and doctors are doing experiments and conducting clinical trials to find safe and effective ways to repair defective genes and the damage they can cause.

At first, scientists focused on inserting a normal copy of a defective or even a missing gene in order to treat inherited disorders. These copies can occur in nature or can be made in a laboratory. Now scientists also are working on broader gene therapies that target cancer, arthritis, and infectious diseases.

With the mapping of the human genome, which was completed in 2003, some people had high hopes for gene therapy and have been disappointed by what they see as a lack of major breakthroughs since then. Trials that fail have attracted more publicity than slow, steady progress toward workable treatments.

KEEPING IT SAFE

IN THE UNITED STATES, THE NATIONAL INSTITUTES OF HEALTH (NIH) PROVIDES GUIDELINES FOR GENE THERAPY RESEARCH BY UNIVERSITIES AND HOSPITALS. IN ADDITION, A SPECIAL NIH COMMITTEE REVIEWS MEDICAL AND ETHICAL CONCERNS. MANY OTHER COUNTRIES HAVE SIMILAR RULES, THOUGH SOME ARE MORE LAX.

TARGETING SINGLE GENE DEFECTS

Scientists have found that defects in a single gene are the easiest to understand and treat. The first successful gene therapy involved a single gene defect that causes severe and often fatal immune deficiency. A four-year-old girl was treated in 1990 and other children subsequently have been helped by experimental gene therapy.

Thousands of researchers are working worldwide to find successful treatments using gene therapy.

Critics of gene therapy believe that it is both inefficient and potentially dangerous because inserted genes could spawn a whole new set of disorders including tumors and cancers. In addition, gene therapy has the potential to stop working quickly as the body learns to defend against the delivery mechanism, particularly if a form of virus has been used.

Despite these concerns, governments and drug companies worldwide are investing billions of dollars in researching and testing gene-based therapies. It is more than likely that these efforts eventually will lead to safe, accessible gene therapy for conditions including cancer, AIDS, cystic fibrosis, circulatory problems, and even blindness and hearing loss.

There are two main types of gene therapy: somatic gene therapy and germline gene therapy. They are differentiated by which kinds of cells are injected with **therapeutic** genes. Although the differences between the two are fairly easy to understand, their effects could have far-reaching and potentially dangerous side effects.

Red blood cells are an example of somatic cells, which are all cells in living organisms that are not involved in sexual reproduction. Some somatic cells circulate in the blood while others need to attach to each other to do their job.

SOMATIC GENE THERAPY

Somatic gene therapy targets somatic cells, which are what people's bodies are made of. This type of gene therapy only affects the person being treated, and is not passed on to future generations. The vast majority of current clinical trials concerning gene therapy are investigating somatic gene therapy. Many genetic diseases are known as single gene disorders, because they're caused by just a single faulty or mutated gene.

These disorders are good candidates for somatic gene therapy, because the treatment would just involve the insertion of a single corrective gene. Diseases of this type in which somatic gene therapies are being looked into as a cure include hemophilia and cystic fibrosis.

Replacing just one gene may not sound too complicated, but scientists have encountered major challenges in their quest for working therapies. First of all, they need to find a carrier that delivers the gene safely to the right spot on the right cells. In a blood disorder such as hemophilia, for example, the target would be bone marrow cells, where red blood cells are made. To treat cystic fibrosis, the deadliest genetic disease, the normal gene would need to reach the lungs and gut, possibly via a nasal spray and some type of swallowed treatment.

Once the delivery challenges have been conquered, scientists will still need to make sure that the new gene stays turned on so the therapy keeps working.

GERMLINE GENE THERAPY

Germline gene therapy involves injecting functional genes into germ cells. These are the cells that are responsible for sexual reproduction, specifically the sperm and egg cells. As a result, any change made to a germ cell will then be passed down to the parents' offspring if and when they reproduce. Many countries, including Canada, Germany, and Australia, have banned research into germline gene therapy for a number of reasons, many of them ethical. For example, it's impossible to know exactly how these inherited genetic changes might affect later generations. With somatic gene therapy, the only person being affected is the person receiving the therapy. However, germline gene therapy could affect several subsequent generations, none of whom consented to or asked for it. For these reasons, and others, there are no clinical trials involving germline gene therapy currently happening. However, there is a large amount of debate about it within the scientific community.

A zygote forms when an egg cell unites with a sperm cell. Researchers in England are studying whether broken mtDNA in a zygote can be replaced with normal mtDNA from a woman who is not the mother. This concept is called the "three-parent baby," but no trials have been conducted yet.

Treating babies before birth with germline gene therapy may sound promising, but it is unclear whether safe therapies ever will exist—and whether they should.

UNKNOWN FUTURE

Scientists concede that there are large gaps in knowledge about germline gene therapy, but many believe it's just a matter of time before answers are found. If that happens, debate about the ethics of this type of therapy would likely intensify amid pressure to allow the use of potentially life-saving new treatments.

CHAPTER 4

GENE THERAPY TECHNIQUES

A number of different methods of gene therapy are currently being developed to help combat genetic disorders. Because different disorders cause problems in different ways, each is treated with a different technique.

GENE AUGMENTATION THERAPY

Some diseases are caused by a cell mutating in such a way that it stops producing what it's supposed to, usually a protein. In these cases, scientists are attempting to use gene augmentation therapy to treat them. A functioning copy of the faulty gene is injected, which replaces the faulty one. Cells are then able to begin making the needed protein.

TWO-WAY APPROACH

GENES CAN BE REPLACED AND REPAIRED BOTH INSIDE (IN VIVO) AND OUTSIDE (EX VIVO) THE BODY. FOR EX VIVO, CELLS WITH DEFECTIVE GENES ARE REMOVED, FIXED IN A LAB, AND RETURNED TO THE BODY. FOR IN VIVO, CORRECTED GENES ARE DELIVERED DIRECTLY TO THE AFFECTED CELLS.

Gene therapy is being tested or considered for treatment of many disorders including immune deficiencies, leukemia and other cancers, HIV, Parkinson's, sickle cell, multiple myeloma, thalassemia, and retinal disease. So far, about 4,000 diseases have been linked to gene defects, but there may be more.

Visitors to the Wellcome Collection, a science and medicine museum in London, can see the first printout of the human genome. It fills up more than 100 books printed in tiny type.

GENE INHIBITION THERAPY

In diseases where the mutated gene causes something harmful to the body to be produced, gene inhibition therapy is used. This technique introduces a gene that either stops the faulty gene from working, or stops what the gene produces from having an effect. This then stops cells that cause disease from growing.

KILLING OF SPECIFIC CELLS

Lastly, some gene therapy targets disease cells directly. DNA is injected into a patient, then enters and kills disease cells. It accomplishes this in one of two ways. In some cases, the DNA will contain a "suicide gene" that manufactures a poisonous product, destroying the cell from within. In others, the inserted DNA produces a protein that makes the disease cell noticeable to the immune system. It is then destroyed by the body's own defenses.

DELIVERY METHODS

There are also multiple ways scientists deliver DNA into cells. The two primary methods use either recombinant viruses or naked DNA.

VIRAL VECTORS

Viruses are basically parasites. They attach to cells and implant them with the virus's DNA. This DNA tells the cell how to make copies of the virus, tricking the cell into using its own production centers to make more and more viruses.

Neurons, or nerve cells, are complex structures that do not regenerate.

SUICIDE GENE

Cells die in one of two ways: necrosis and apoptosis. Necrosis occurs when a cell becomes damaged by injury or infection and dies. This can be a messy and painful process for the organism. Apoptosis, in contrast, is a natural process of cell death orchestrated by an organism to get rid of aging and unhealthy cells by cutting off supplies to them. A visible example of this is the way skin cells die off and are replaced by newly generated ones. Not all cells undergo this process, though. Some somatic cells, particularly neurons, or nerve cells, cannot regenerate. This makes it very difficult to heal from injuries involving nerves or the spine.

Cancer is another major challenge to modern medicine, and that is why scientists are testing the use of suicide genes to combat it. The modified gene ultimately convinces the cancer cells to shut themselves down. Initial trials have reported some promising results.

Recombinant viruses are made in laboratories by splicing together different strands of DNA. This allows scientists to replace the virus' DNA with genes that are designed to help correct issues in a patent's genome. Once injected, the virus acts as it normally would, only it's getting the host cells to make copies of therapeutic genes instead of the harmful viral DNA. Viruses that are designed for this purpose are called viral **vectors**. A number of different types of viruses have proven useful for delivering therapeutic DNA, including retroviruses and adenoviruses.

NON-VIRAL DELIVERY

There are a number of methods for introducing genes that don't involve viruses. These have a few advantages over using viral vectors. For one, they have a lower chance of triggering an immune response from the body. Because viruses are foreign agents, they are often targeted by the body's immune system for destruction, which can limit their effectiveness. Materials for these methods are often easier to produce on a larger scale, as well. However, there are also drawbacks.

Some forms of gene therapy can be administered via injection into intramuscular tissue. Patients are generally familiar with this type of treatment.

Without a virus, the new genes often have trouble spreading and replicating across cells. Also, the genes might have a harder time being read, and therefore might not be able to achieve what they were meant to do. New technology has helped deal with these last two issues in recent years, though.

Injection of naked DNA, usually into intramuscular tissue, is the simplest non-viral delivery method. However, the gene's ability to express itself, or perform its function, hasn't proven as effective as with viral methods. Because of this, researchers are looking into both physical and chemical ways to improve the delivery of naked DNA into cells. These include using ultrasonic frequencies to penetrate cell walls, and even a "gene gun," which uses gold particles to "shoot" DNA into cells.

ONGOING RESEARCH

Gene therapy is likely to improve by leaps and bounds over the next years as scientists perfect delivery methods and learn how to treat more disorders. These advances may include:

- Using bacterial or viral genes as a new form of vaccination.

- Destroying or neutralizing cancer cells with gene therapy that would be safer, easier, and more effective than current treatments.

- Using genes to stimulate production of new or regenerated tissues, particularly in cases of damage to the brain, spine, or nerves.

CHAPTER 5
CHALLENGES WITH GENE THERAPY

Currently, gene therapy is not a widely used treatment. Because it's still so new, scientists are still attempting to come up with safe ways to use it that work consistently for most patients afflicted with a disorder. Research into gene therapy is also highly regulated in most countries, which means that research has to be done to very precise standards. As a result, studies into new therapies often move along very slowly.

Many genetic disorders are incredibly rare. Some only affect a few dozen people in the entire world. Because of this, therapies involving these conditions often aren't investigated. This is both because researchers want to look into ways of helping the most people possible, and because it's hard for companies to turn a profit on a therapy that can only be sold to 50 people worldwide.

RISKY CURE

IT TAKES MANY YEARS TO DETERMINE LONG-TERM SAFETY OF MEDICAL TREATMENTS, AND GENE THERAPY IS QUITE NEW. EVEN SO, SCIENTISTS TRY TO MAKE CLINICAL TRIALS AS SAFE AS POSSIBLE. IN MANY TRIALS, PARTICIPANTS ARE SO ILL THAT THEY ARE WILLING TO ACCEPT THE RISK.

Gene therapy products are regulated by the Food and Drug Administration (FDA) in the United States and by similar agencies in many other countries. The FDA must approve all clinical trials. When products are ready for public use, the FDA must approve that as well. The agency also monitors for adverse effects and can shut down a trial or take a product off the market.

Within the FDA, the Center for Biologics Evaluation and Research monitors genetic and cellular therapies.

31

Researchers have also had issues with getting treatments to last. Many cells divide so rapidly that new genes can't take hold, and the treatments stop working. Much research is being done into how to make a long-lasting change to the genome that will solve the issues presented by a disorder, without adverse effects.

AVAILABILITY

Almost all gene therapy is available only in clinical studies in the United States. The exception is Imlygic, a treatment for melanoma, which became the first gene therapy approved by the FDA in late 2015. There are currently hundreds of clinical trials taking place. These are attempting to treat not just traditional genetic disorders, but also diseases such as cancer and HIV/AIDS.

Clinical trials are a stage of research that all new drugs go through. It's important to determine that treatments are able to do what they claim, and do it in a safe way. Clinical trials help in this process by testing the therapy on volunteers who have been informed of its possible dangers and possible benefits. They also help determine exactly what dosage should be used when it is given.

Clinical trials take place in three steps. In phase one, the main goal is to determine dosage amounts. In phase two, effectiveness is examined, in a larger pool of patients.

When other treatments fail, patients often choose to volunteer for one of hundreds of ongoing gene therapy trials.

If the results are promising, phase three begins. Phase three aims to see if the treatment is more effective than other commonly available treatments. If the therapy being tested is the only treatment for a particular disorder or disease, it's tested against a placebo, a treatment that doesn't actually contain any medicine.

For many genetic disorders, there are no currently available treatments. This means that a patient's best option might be a clinical trial. It's up to each individual patient to determine if the benefits outweigh the potential risks. Volunteers are told of any adverse effects that have presented in animal trials. However, because animals and humans react to things differently, there is always the potential for additional, unforeseen risks. For some people, the chance at a cure or a more effective treatment will trump the fear of unknown side effects. Some are willing to be subjected to the dangers of new treatments so that patients in future trials might benefit. Others might not want to put themselves at risk. It all comes down to the individual.

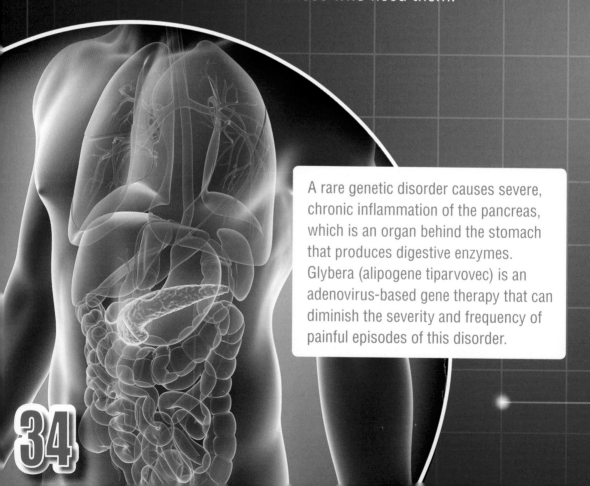

Another obstacle in the way of wide availability of gene therapy is cost. Many treatments are very expensive. The first gene therapy product approved for sale in Europe was Glybera, in 2012. It was developed to treat a rare enzyme deficiency. However, each treatment cost about $1 million. In August 2016, it was announced that a gene therapy treatment that could cure ADA-SCID, a deadly immune disorder, would cost $665,000 when released in Europe. There are a few reasons for this, including the difficulty in making the treatments, and the often low numbers of affected people. However, these astronomical costs mean that even when gene therapies are available, they are still often out of reach of those who need them.

A rare genetic disorder causes severe, chronic inflammation of the pancreas, which is an organ behind the stomach that produces digestive enzymes. Glybera (alipogene tiparvovec) is an adenovirus-based gene therapy that can diminish the severity and frequency of painful episodes of this disorder.

Adenoviruses make good vectors for gene therapy because there are lots of them and they usually cause only mild cold symptoms. They are also large enough to hold fairly long segments of DNA.

RISKS

Gene therapy trials still hold a number of potential risks. This is one of the main reasons clinical studies are so important. These risks need to be identified and, if possible, eliminated before gene therapies are made widely available.

The fact that viruses are often used as delivery mechanisms for therapeutic DNA has led to a number of issues. There is the danger of an immune response. This is because the body's immune system is built to attack viruses. As a result, sometimes the body attacks the virus before it can do its job. This immune response can have negative side effects, such as inflammation or even organ failure. The immune system also learns how to fend off viruses better the more it deals with them. This presents a problem if a therapy depends on multiple doses of the same recombinant virus.

It's also possible for the virus to affect cells other than the ones it was meant to target. This could cause the death of healthy cells, which could have a serious negative impact.

There's also a chance the virus could revert to a form which causes disease. This could cause an unintended and harmful infection.

Another risk is triggering a tumor. If genes are inserted into the wrong spot, like in a sequence that suppresses tumors, it could turn that gene off. This has occasionally been an issue in some clinical trials.

Gene therapy has even rarely caused the death of patients involved in clinical trials. The most famous of these was the case of Jesse Gelsinger. Gelsinger suffered from a rare genetic disease that affected his liver. After being injected with an adenoviral vector, he suffered a massive, unforeseen immune response. This led to multiple organ failures, including lung and kidney shutdown, and brain death. He died four days after receiving the injection. His death in 1999 was the first in the world to be linked to gene therapy research.

These risks also highlight the importance of informed consent in clinical trials. It's important that everyone volunteering for a trial realize how dangerous the treatment might be, so they can make up their own mind about whether or not to participate. It's not enough to tell patients about known side effects. They also need to be told that there's a chance of completely unforeseen consequences arising. This is exactly why clinical trials are so heavily monitored and regulated. Without strict oversight the potential for harm could increase dramatically.

Specialists in medical ethics continue to meet worldwide to discuss evolving concerns about gene therapy.

ETHICAL ISSUES SURROUNDING GENE THERAPY

Aside from the medical problems that need to be solved in relation to gene therapy, there are also many ethical issues that are currently being debated. Germline gene therapy is a major focus of these debates. Because it alters genes that are then passed down to future generations, it inspires a number of questions. Will it have unforeseen consequences for descendants of the original patient? Could an alteration to germ cells affect a growing fetus? Should preventative treatment be given to people who haven't yet been born, and therefore can't consent?

There are many other issues. What exactly constitutes a genetic disorder? It could be said that shortness is a disadvantage. Should gene therapy be used to correct it? Because gene therapy is currently so expensive, should it only be available to the rich? These and many other questions are hotly debated by scientists, philosophers, and everyday people.

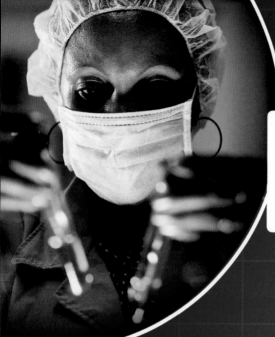

So much research is needed that many new jobs are becoming available in the field of gene therapy research. Years of advanced training are required, usually including a medical or doctoral degree.

LAST RESORT FOR NOW

Because of the myriad issues surrounding gene therapy, including the high cost, the difficulty in producing therapies, and the risks associated with testing, it is currently only being researched as a treatment for conditions with no other known cure. Also, the benefits of therapy must outweigh any possible negative consequences. For example, temporary hair loss, though a negative side effect, is considered acceptable if the therapy also cures a potentially deadly disorder. Huge strides have been made in understanding how individual genes work and how they might be used to treat devastating disorders and diseases. However, there is still much more research to be done before gene therapy is a widespread practice. Important research is being conducted into how risks can be lessened or eliminated. Many are working to bring down the cost of treatment. If these hurdles can be overcome, the potential of gene therapy is awe-inspiring.

FIGHTING CANCER

Cancer is one of the deadliest and most feared diseases among humans. The treatments can be brutal with severe side effects such as hair loss, weight loss, and painful nausea.

Scientists are excited about several potential treatments including using gene therapy to create cancer vaccines. Many consider a new gene-editing technique called CRISPR to be especially promising. CRISPR easily finds the target gene, locks on, and delivers the edited gene to the right place. It can do this because it is made from RNA, which can be custom-designed to match a strip of DNA. Scientists learned to do this from watching how bacteria invade!

CRISPR also has the advantage of being able to target more than one gene at the same time. Though there are still challenges to overcome, many researchers believe CRISPR will help them to make cancer treatment breakthroughs.

GENE THERAPY OF THE FUTURE

As more and more trials progress, it's becoming clearer hich gene therapy treatments seem to be working. There are handful of disorders that scientists are hoping can soon be eated or even cured with these revolutionary techniques.

Hemophilia has long been a candidate for gene therapy cause relatively few cells need to receive new DNA for eatment to be effective. One study found that half of the cipients of gene therapy to treat their hemophilia had lessened mptoms. Once this treatment is refined, it could be used to eat hemophilia, and even provide important data to treat other ood disorders, such as sickle-cell disease.

Eye disease is another major focus for gene therapy ing forward. This is because there are over 150 hereditary ngle-gene defects that can cause the retina to degrade. ngle-gene disorders are good candidates for gene therapy cause only one gene needs to be corrected.

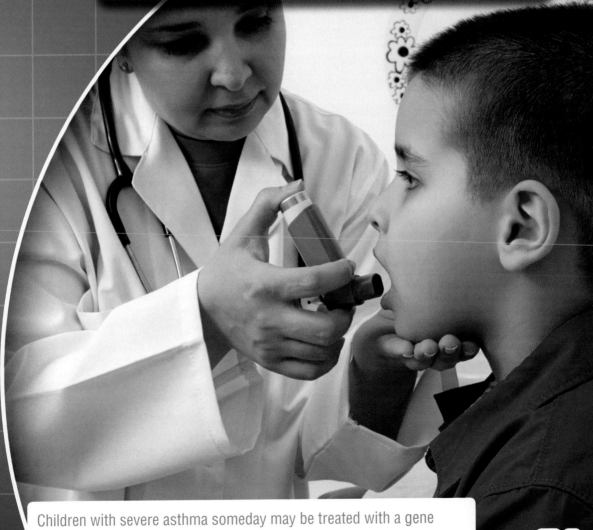

No matter what gene therapies are discovered, scientists also must focus on making them last.

To avoid the need for repeated treatments, the cells receiving therapeutic DNA ideally should have a long, stable life. Many cells, though, divide rapidly and go through apoptosis. The affected tissues eventually die and are replaced. Scientists need to find a way around this to create gene therapies that are not short-lived.

Children with severe asthma someday may be treated with a gene therapy based on tiny DNA nanoparticles that repair damaged airways. The therapy has been tested successfully, but so far only on mice.

41

The eye is a good test subject for gene therapy for a few reasons. Firstly, eyes are good test subjects because they don't have many immune cells. Therapy will not provoke a dangerous immune response.

It's also accessible, so the retina, a part of the eye that reflects light, can be targeted with precision. A genetic therapy has been found to help one inherited type of blindness and could win FDA approval soon.

Researchers are also busy coming up with new ways to use gene therapy to combat diseases that might involve multiple genes, as well as environmental causes. Cancer is an obvious candidate. One promising technique involves removing **T-cells** from the blood and giving them a gene that makes a protein that specifically targets tumor cells. The T-cells are then put back into the bloodstream. This method has been very successful in trials, and it's hoped that it can be adapted to fight a variety of cancers.

T-cells also factor into an experimental gene therapy used to combat HIV. HIV replicates inside of T-cells. However, T-cells need to have a functioning CCR5, a cell-surface receptor, for HIV to get inside. Researchers have been able to remove T-cells and give them a gene that alters their CCR5, so that it won't allow HIV to enter. HIV-positive patients who received this treatment in a trial showed anti-HIV effects when taken off of medications.

A T-cell does not get its name from the letter T, but rather from the fact that T-cells mature in the thymus gland and sometimes in the tonsils. This type of white blood cell controls much of the body's immune response.

GENETIC ENGINEERING

There is also the potential to use gene therapy to change traits in humans that have nothing to do with health. One example would be altering a fetus's genes to make sure it has blue eyes. While that might seem harmless, it creates a slippery ethical slope. What traits are desirable, and which aren't? Who would decide that?

There are many possible applications for this. Experiments have already used gene therapy to create mice that can eat more food without gaining weight, can run for longer periods of time before getting tired, and are stronger. One study managed to grow mice with improved memory by adding an extra copy of the NR2B gene to embryos.

Imagine if you could become thinner, stronger, faster, and smarter, just by getting a shot. Or if you could design everything about your baby before it was born, from exactly how it would look to how intelligent it would be. While this might seem great, it would have potentially harmful consequences. What if the shots were so expensive only the rich could afford them? What would happen to those who couldn't? If a designer baby doesn't actually share any of your genes, is it really yours? And in a world where physical and mental perfection are so easily attained, what purpose is there to try for anything?

If there's one truth to human history, it's that technology almost always marches on. Humanity is going to figure out the answers to these questions eventually, and maybe sooner than anybody thought. Gene therapy could solve countless problems that humanity has struggled with for millennia. But humans will also have to deal with new problems that these amazing solutions create.

TIMELINE OF GENE THERAPY DEVELOPMENT

Scientists present the concept of gene therapy as a solution for genetic disorders in the journal *Science*.

1972

Frederich Miescher discovers nuclein, later renamed DNA.

1869

Fist approved gene therapy trial is conducted on a four-year-old girl with an immune disease. Results are still in question today.

1990

James Watson and Francis Crick are the first to describe the structure of DNA, accurately identifying it as a double helix.

1953

1980

Martin Cline attempts the first human gene therapy trial using rDNA. Doing so, he breaks multiple regulations and defies the committees overseeing his work. It is unsuccessful and Cline's reputation is ruined.

Jesse Gelsinger becomes
the first patient to die as
a direct result of a clinical
trial of gene therapy.

1999

2012

Europe approves
Glybera, the first gene
therapy product in
the Western world.
The cost is generally
prohibitively high.

2014

Trials treating
certain blood and
eye disorders, as
well as HIV, show
promise.

2003

First commercial
gene therapy
treatment is approved
in China for various
forms of cancer.

2015

The US FDA approved
T-VEC, under the brand
name Imlygic, for the
treatment of melanoma
in patients with
inoperable tumors.

2002

Cancer is discovered in
patients being treated
for the immune disease
SCID-X1.

GLOSSARY

bacteria: Single-celled organisms that are rod, spiral, or sphere shaped, some of which can cause disease.

defective: Not working properly.

disease: A condition that affects living things and prevents them from functioning as well as they're normally able to.

enzyme: A specific type of protein that causes a certain chemical change.

fetus: The state of development in human offspring that begins eight weeks after conception.

molecule: A unit made up of at least two atoms. It is the furthest anything can be broken down while still retaining recognizable characteristics and chemical properties.

mutation: A sudden, spontaneous change in an organism's genetic material.

organism: A living thing such as a plant, animal, or even a single-celled life-form.

proteins: Organic compounds made up of molecules that are formed by chains of amino acids.

T-cells: A type of white blood cell that helps the immune system by recognizing and identifying foreign cells in the body.

therapeutic: Possessing properties that heal disease.

vector: A molecule that carries and delivers DNA into a cell. Viruses can infect anything, from humans all the way down to a single bacterium.

virus: A kind of tiny parasite that can only replicate in living cells of other organisms.

FOR MORE INFORMATION

BOOKS

Carmichael, L. E. *Gene Therapy.*
Edina, MN: ABDO Publishing Company, 2013.

Lloyd Kyi, Tanya. *DNA Detective.* Toronto, ON: Annick Press, 2015.

Mooney, Carla. *Genetics.*
White River Junction, VT: Nomad Press, 2014.

WEBSITES

https://ghr.nlm.nih.gov/primer/therapy/genetherapy
U.S. National Library of Medicine

**http://www.mensaforkids.org/teach/lesson-plans/
peas-in-a-pod-genetics/**
Mensa Education & Research Foundation—Genetics

Publisher's note to educators and parents: Our editors have carefully reviewed these websites to ensure that they are suitable for students. Many websites change frequently, however, and we cannot guarantee that a site's future contents will continue to meet our high standards of quality and educational value. Be advised that students should be closely supervised whenever they access the Internet.

INDEX